101 Management Tips

Mostafa Maleki Tehrani

F
x
M

Firouz Media 2024

Firouz Media Limited have contributed to the publication of this book, while the author retains full responsibility for copyright, content accuracy, and any legal matters. This book is a testament to the author's commitment and enthusiasm, and our involvement represents a collaborative hybrid effort in publishing. As you immerse yourself in its contents, we sincerely hope you find inspiration, insight, and delight.

ISBN 978-1-915557-21-6
www.firouzmedia.com
IG: @firouzmedia

Cover picture: Tuomas Kujansuu
Stock images: Pexels_Adobe_Pixabay

101 Management Tips
Creator: Mostafa Maleki Tehrani

Preface

Management is one of the sciences that all humans encounter at every moment. The way a child interact with their parents is the first managerial step that every individual takes involuntarily, and after that, they become involved in the subject at every moment. Interactions with parents, family, spouse, children, and colleagues all derive from the fundamental principles of management. If we learn the basic principles of this science, we define relationships with others based on win-win situations; otherwise, our human and emotional relationships are affected by the coldness of relationships, turning their constructive impact into a destructive factor for the soul and body.

Regardless of its type and level, management requires continuous review of materials that may be very simple but important at the same time. Many managers become entangled in the bureaucracy of their organizations, missing this important opportunity. In this book, an attempt has been made to present 101 important tips for managers in a simple, explicit, and illustrative manner, so that with a quick and daily glance, these points become ingrained in the mind.

A very important point is that management is not summarized in these tips, so I have tried to prepare and present the most important and simplest tips in various areas such as human resources, strategy, and finance. It's undeniable that experts and scholars in the realm of management might challenge certain viewpoints while validating others. The breadth of this field is vast, suggesting that its boundaries are virtually limitless. Thus, I reiterate that while understanding these 101 tips is essential, it alone is not adequate for effective management.

—Mostafa Maleki Tehrani

1

Building network and establishing connections in a company becomes beneficial when it involves the aggregation of measurable capabilities present within the organization.

Networking within a company connects individuals, teams, and departments to leverage their collective capabilities and resources. "Aggregation of measurable capabilities" combines quantifiable skills, expertise, and resources, both tangible and intangible. This approach enhances overall performance by fostering collaboration, efficiency, innovation, informed decision-making, and competitiveness.

2

Correct thinking in the right position means transforming an idea into a product, just like Edison did.

In Edison's case, he didn't just conceive groundbreaking concepts; he strategically positioned himself in a time and place where his inventions could make a significant impact. His work on the electric light bulb, phonograph, and motion pictures, among others, revolutionized various industries. The phrase suggests that the success of an idea is not only dependent on its quality but also on its timing, relevance, and practical implementation. So, "transforming an idea into a product, like Edison," highlights the need for strategic thinking, proper execution, and aligning innovative concepts with the right circumstances to achieve meaningful results.

Courtesy of ImageFlow

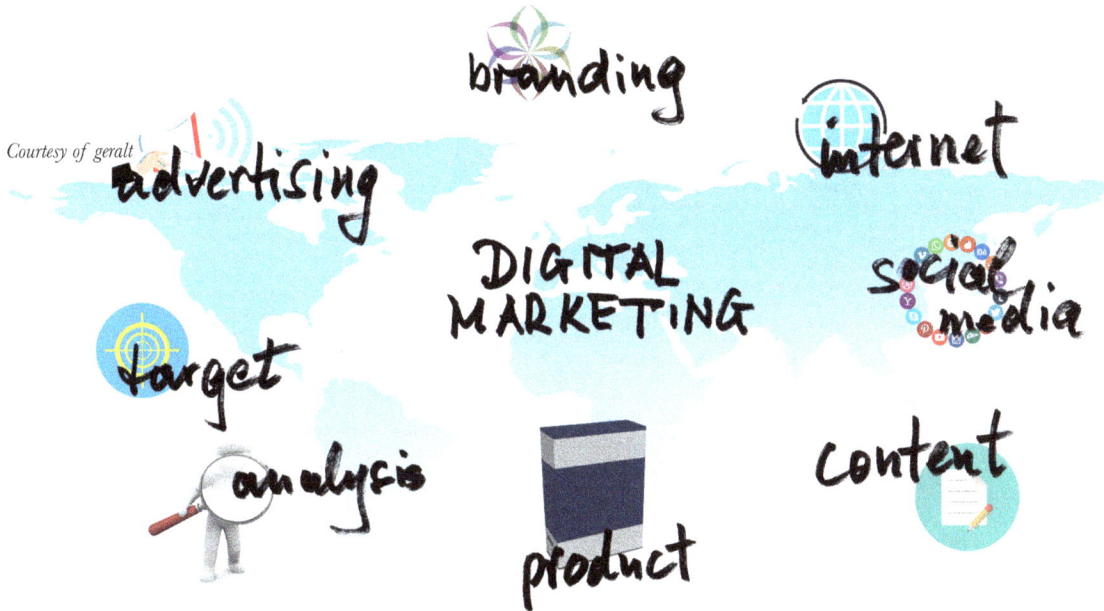
Courtesy of geralt

3

International manufacturing means turning countries into brands, like Toyota.

This highlights the global reach and impact of manufacturing companies that have successfully established themselves as industry leaders on an international scale. Toyota, for instance, is not only a car manufacturer but also a symbol of quality, innovation, and reliability worldwide. By consistently delivering high-quality products and services across borders, such companies transcend national boundaries and become synonymous with excellence in their respective industries.

4

If you lack a significant piece of the puzzle, don't venture into it, like aircraft manufacturing.

This analogy suggests that if you are missing a crucial component or expertise in a particular area, it's better to refrain from entering that field, much like the complexity and precision required in aircraft manufacturing. It emphasizes the importance of having all the necessary resources and capabilities before embarking on a new venture or project.

Courtesy of johnhain

5

Having identical puzzle pieces doesn't serve the purpose, just like a community with doctors but lacking artists.

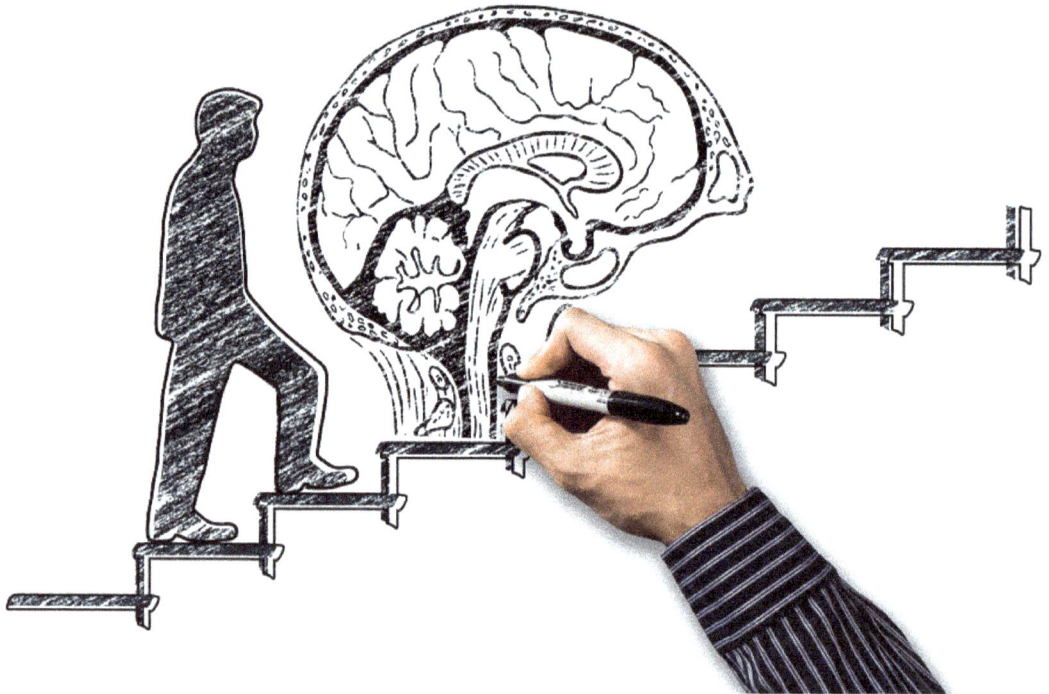

Courtesy of geralt

6

Establish a platform dedicated to nurturing the growth and refinement of knowledge and skills.

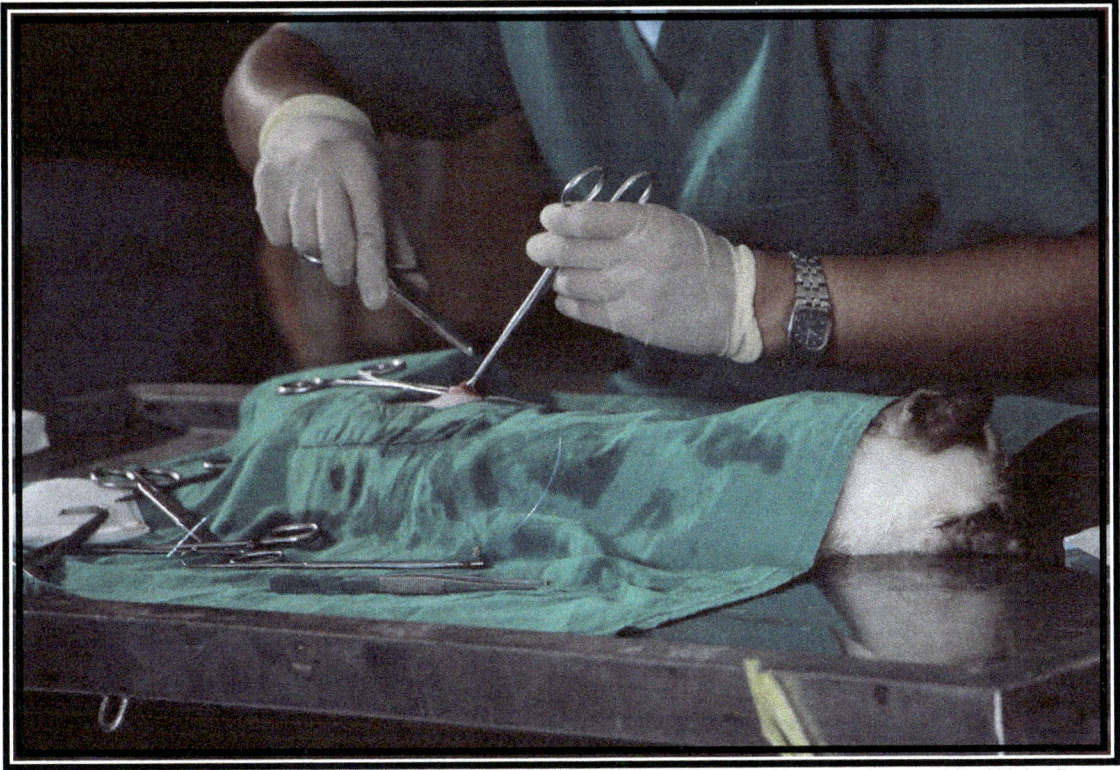

7

Skills as important as knowledge; a doctor requires skills.

In the realm of management, the emphasis on skills over knowledge underscores the importance of practical expertise and proficiency in executing tasks effectively. While knowledge provides the foundation and understanding of concepts, skills are what enable individuals to apply that knowledge in real-world situations.

Courtesy of fauxels

8

The process of creating a good product is time-consuming and requires tools, skills, and an execution team.

9

For creating a complex product, global expertise is necessary, and different tools, skills, and expertise are required, such as building a spacecraft.

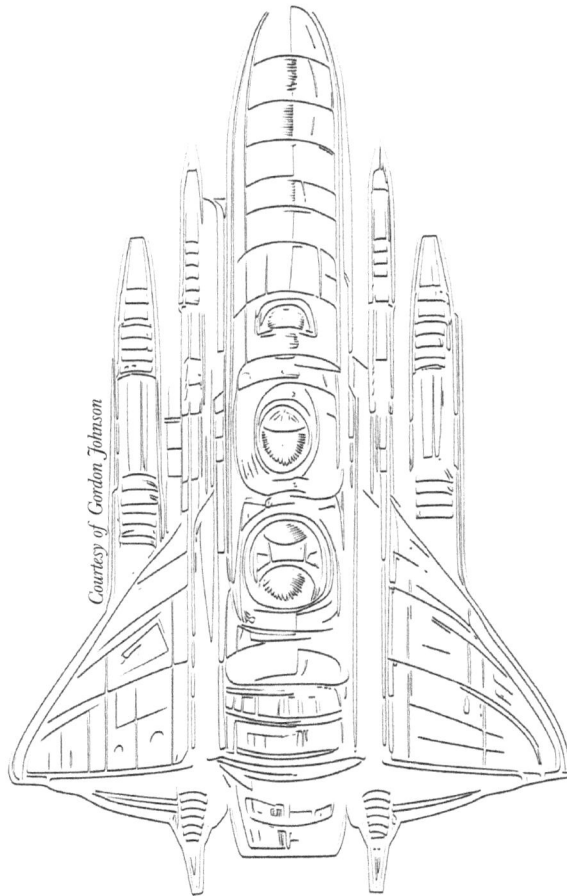

Courtesy of Gordon Johnson

10

Avoid ubiquitous products to avoid stagnation.

From a management perspective, it's crucial to steer clear of ubiquitous products to avoid getting stuck in a rut. When a product is overly common and lacks differentiation, it becomes challenging to stand out in the market and capture the attention of customers.

11

If we surpass the defined border of knowledge and skill, we have created a difference.

This statement suggests that when individuals go beyond the traditional limitations of either knowledge or skill, they distinguish themselves from others. From a management perspective, it highlights the importance of fostering a culture of continuous learning and development within an organization. By encouraging employees to expand their knowledge and hone their skills, managers can empower them to achieve excellence and stand out in their respective fields. This can lead to increased innovation, productivity, and competitiveness for the organization as a whole.

Courtesy of Art30405

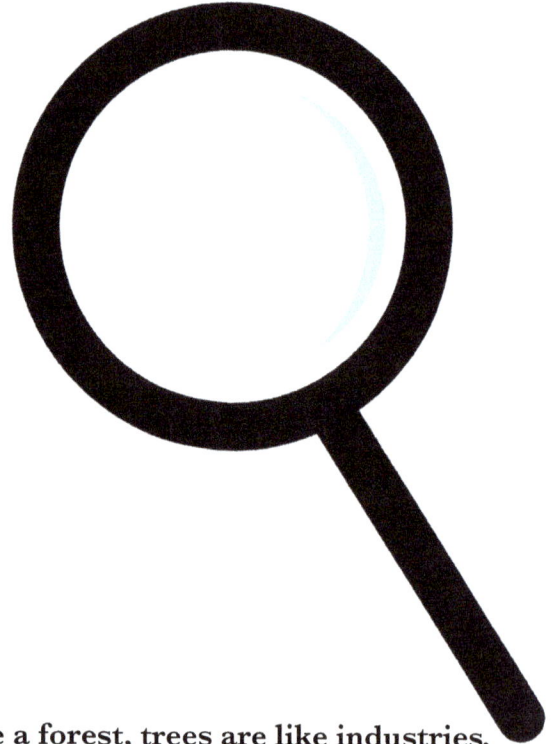

Courtesy of FunkyFocus

12

In an efficient system, the economy is like a forest, trees are like industries, monkeys are like factories, and companies are like fruits and products.

This metaphor illustrates the interconnectedness and productivity of various elements within an efficient economic system, highlighting how each component plays a vital role in sustaining the overall ecosystem.

13

For different industries, different patterns are required, so that trial and error can be minimized.

Each industry has its unique characteristics and requirements, and therefore, it's necessary to adopt different approaches or patterns tailored to each industry's specific needs. By doing so, the need for trial and error, which can be time-consuming and costly, is minimized.

Courtesy of Sanctumdigital

14

The shortest distance to the product means the highest profit; the strongest connection means the best product.

Minimizing production steps boosts profit; strong relationships lead to superior products, emphasizing efficiency and customer focus for business success.

15

It's a good idea if it can be executed.

Having a good idea is only valuable if it can be put into action effectively. In other words, while creativity and innovation are important, practical implementation is equally crucial for success.

Courtesy of Mediamodifier

Courtesy of MMT OREL

16

Building motivation or undermining it is contagious.

Both fostering motivation and sabotaging it can have a ripple effect. When motivation is created, it tends to spread among individuals, inspiring them to work harder and achieve their goals. Similarly, when motivation is destroyed or undermined, it can spread negativity and demotivation throughout a group or organization. Therefore, it underscores the importance of cultivating a positive environment and mindset to foster motivation and drive success.

17

The fit between an individual and a job is the masterpiece of human resources.

Courtesy of Tumisu

18

For unstructured jobs, innate qualities greatly impact performance.

Consider a role in sales, where there's often a degree of ambiguity and unpredictability in interactions with clients and leads. In such unstructured jobs, individuals with innate qualities like charisma, adaptability, and strong communication skills often excel. These traits enable them to build rapport with clients, navigate uncertain situations effectively, and persuade others, ultimately driving sales success.

Courtesy of Clem Onojeghuo

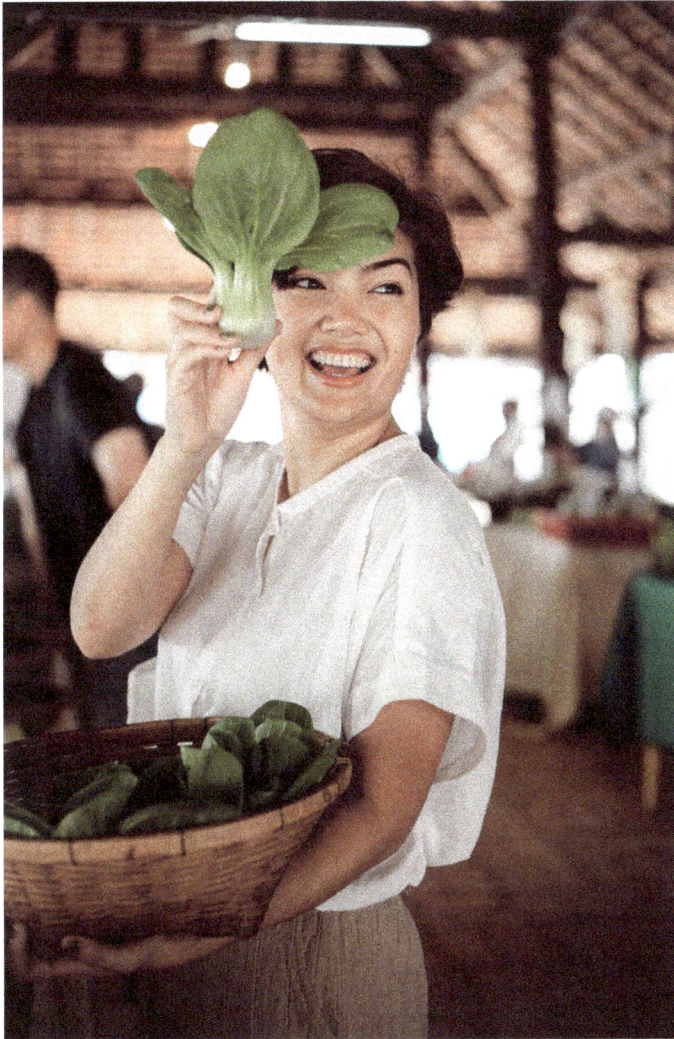
Courtesy of Sam Lion

19

The positive impact on customer satisfaction differs from the sales index.

A high sales index doesn't always mean high customer satisfaction if other factors like service quality are lacking.

Courtesy of Kampus Production

20

Similar training doesn't always have the same effect on employee performance.

Factors such as prior experience, natural aptitude, and willingness to learn can influence how employees internalize and apply the training content, leading to different outcomes in their performance.

Courtesy of Cottonbro studio

21

Low productivity occurs due to three reasons: not knowing, not being able to, and not wanting to.

low productivity is attributed to a combination of factors related to knowledge, ability, and motivation. Addressing these factors through training, skill development programs, and fostering a positive work environment can help improve productivity levels.

22

When personnel know but don't want to, it signifies the presence of discrimination.

Employers have a responsibility to create a positive work environment where all employees feel valued, motivated, and empowered to perform their best. Addressing issues of discrimination or inequality through fair policies, transparent communication, and opportunities for professional development can help foster a culture of inclusivity and maximize employee potential.

When employees possess the knowledge or skills to perform their tasks effectively but lack the motivation or willingness to do so, it can indicate a form of discrimination or unfair treatment within the workplace.

Courtesy of Cottonbro

23

Clarify expectations for human resources.

Employers need to clarify expectations for personnel to ensure alignment, performance management, productivity, engagement, and retention.

Courtesy of Fauxels

Courtesy of Gerd Altmann

24

Downswing doesn't happen overnight.

Understanding that downturns develop gradually allows managers to anticipate, plan for, and mitigate risks effectively, fostering adaptability, strategic planning, and transparent communication within the organization.

Courtesy of Guggenberger_Et

25

More important than the job itself, the job's reward, or its social status, is the volume and significance of it.

A job's impact goes beyond its tangible benefits, encompassing the importance of the role itself, workload, work-life balance, job security, social support, and sense of purpose, all affecting an individual's well-being.

Courtesy of Aman Jakhar

26

Identify the factors that contribute to individual job attachment, improve them, and thereby increase productivity.

Courtesy of Ron Lach

27

Ensure that employees have access to tools, facilities, resources, information, and other necessities to perform their jobs effectively and provide them as needed.

Courtesy of Gerd Altmann

28

Investing in employees' growth and development not only fosters their progress and creates a sense of security, but also facilitates the organization's advancement.

Courtesy of Gerd Altmann

29

It's crucial to acknowledge and value the thoughts, ideas, initiatives, and suggestions of employees.

By actively listening to their input and welcoming their contributions, organizations can foster a culture of collaboration, innovation, and continuous improvement. This not only empowers employees to feel heard and appreciated but also harnesses the collective intelligence and creativity of the workforce, leading to better decision-making and organizational success.

Courtesy of OpenClipart-Vectors

30

Empower employees by ensuring they understand the significant role they play in the organization's success.

Courtesy of Gerd Altmann

31

Encourage employees to seek out a workplace culture that prioritizes ethics and values, and collaborate with colleagues who share those same principles.

" Promoting a workplace culture centered on ethics and values and teaming up with like-minded colleagues cultivates an atmosphere of trust and integrity, fostering better collaboration and teamwork, which in turn boosts performance and productivity. Empowering employees through clarity about their role's importance in the organization's success enhances engagement and motivation. When employees feel appreciated and empowered, they tend to excel, thereby aiding in achieving organizational objectives. Such a positive culture not only draws top talent but also keeps current employees, resulting in a united and high-performing team. "

Courtesy of Gerd Altmann

Courtesy of Fauxels

32

Consider arranging a consensus meeting in your workplace to discuss values and principles, fostering dialogue, comprehension, and alignment among team members.

This initiative can enhance cohesion and collaboration within the team, contributing to a more harmonious and productive work environment.

33

Effective supervision ensures that employees are clear about their responsibilities and expectations.

Courtesy of Gerd Altmann

34

Conversation and negotiation are different; conversation aims for a win-win outcome, while negotiation may result in a win-lose scenario. Engage in conversations with employees to persuade them and make their work more appealing.

Courtesy of Gerd Altmann

35

Eliminate the excuse of not knowing from employees.

Courtesy of Anıl Görkem Özşan

To eliminate the excuse of not knowing from employees:

- Communicate clearly through various channels.
- Provide comprehensive training.
- Encourage open feedback.
- Maintain accessible documentation.
- Hold employees accountable.
- Schedule regular check-ins.
- Lead by example in seeking clarity and understanding.

These steps create a culture of clarity and accountability, reducing the likelihood of employees using "not knowing" as an excuse.

36

Address the issue of employee inability head-on to foster accountability and productivity in the workplace.

Courtesy of Cottonbro studio

Courtesy of Johannes Plenio

37

Encourage personnel to follow up on tasks or issues promptly, as their proactive approach signifies the significance of the matter at hand.

Courtesy of Monstera Production

38

By allocating time for conversations with employees, managers demonstrate the importance they place on their team members.

The "Pay to Quit" policy at Amazon is significant because it:

- Aligns employees with the company's mission.
- Retains more engaged workers.
- Saves costs in the long run.
- Reinforces a high-performance culture.
- Provides flexibility in workforce management.

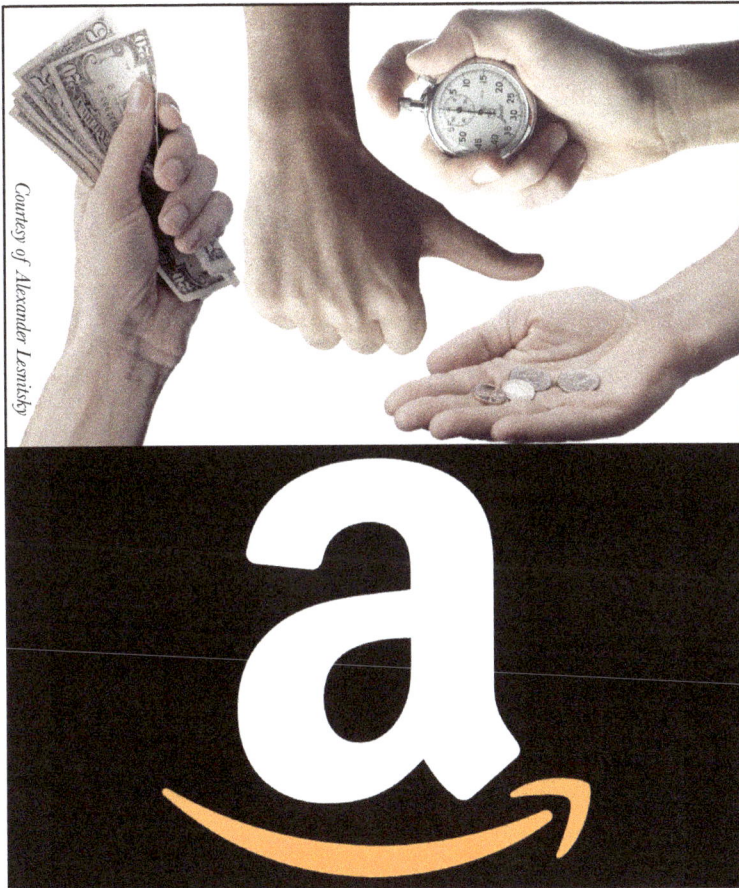

Courtesy of Alexander Lesnitsky

39

Consider implementing a "Pay to Quit" model like Amazon's, where employees are offered money to voluntarily leave their positions.

40

Prioritizing the enforcement and updating of rules is vital.

It ensures consistency and compliance throughout the organization while providing clear guidance to employees. By adapting rules to changing circumstances, management can maintain agility and responsiveness. Moreover, it helps mitigate risks associated with non-compliance and fosters a culture of accountability and trust among employees.

Courtesy of Sora Shimazaki

Courtesy of Sora Shimazaki

41

Avoid engaging in favoritism or nepotism when structuring and making decisions within the organization.

Such practices can undermine morale, breed resentment among employees, and damage trust in leadership. Additionally, they can lead to missed opportunities for talent development and hinder diversity and inclusion efforts. Prioritizing merit-based decisions ensures that the organization benefits from the diverse skills and perspectives of all employees, ultimately contributing to its success and sustainability.

42

Ensure a workplace free from hypocrisy to maintain trust and integrity within the organization.

43

Before implementing a policy, ensure it's feasible and sustainable by assessing resources and potential challenges.

Conducting a comprehensive analysis helps mitigate the risk of unforeseen issues arising and increases the likelihood of successful policy implementation.

Courtesy of succo

44

In highly mature organizations, utilizing effective tools can lead to higher performance levels.

Utilizing effective tools in highly mature organizations can significantly enhance performance. These tools may include advanced software systems, streamlined processes, sophisticated analytics, and cutting-edge technologies. By leveraging such tools, organizations can improve efficiency, decision-making, and overall productivity. Additionally, these tools enable better data management, collaboration, and innovation, driving continuous improvement and competitive advantage. Investing in the right tools and ensuring their optimal utilization is essential for maintaining and furthering the success of highly mature organizations.

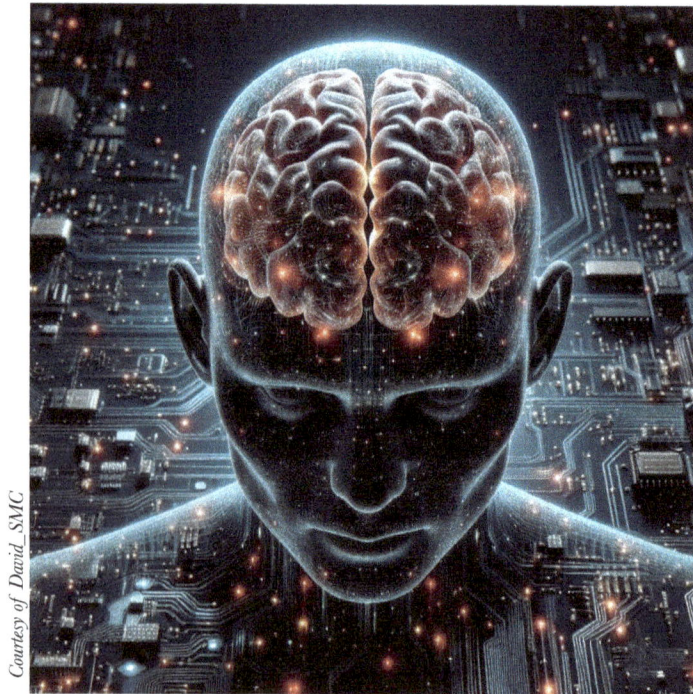

Courtesy of David_SMC

45

To ensure successful implementation, prioritize laws and regulations that are economically viable.

Courtesy of David_SMC

Courtesy of Flo Dahm

46

If social insecurity spills over into the natural environment, work conditions can become increasingly challenging for management.

The environment in which employees work significantly impacts their performance, well-being, and overall satisfaction. When social issues affect the physical workspace or surroundings, it compounds the challenges faced by management in maintaining a productive and harmonious work environment. Therefore, addressing social insecurities and ensuring a positive, supportive atmosphere within both the social and physical aspects of the workplace is crucial for effective management.

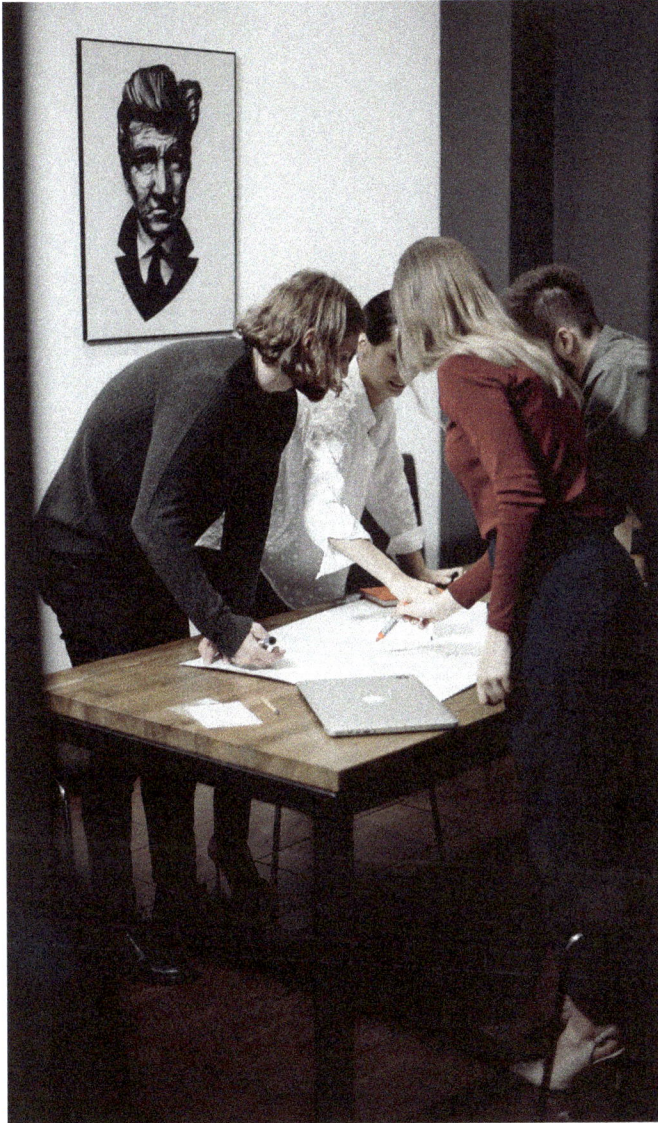
Courtesy of Cottonbro studio

47

To increase organizational efficiency, we need improvement, adjustment, paradigm shift, and even revolution, but ultimately if we fail to achieve these goals, we may need to reform the organizational structure.

These efforts are aimed at driving meaningful transformation and improvement across the organization. However, if despite these endeavors, the desired outcomes are not achieved, it may become necessary to reconsider and reform the fundamental structure of the organization itself. This could involve restructuring departments, redefining roles and responsibilities, or even reshaping the organizational hierarchy to better align with the organization's goals and objectives. Ultimately, the goal is to ensure that the structure of the organization supports and facilitates its overall success and effectiveness.

Courtesy of Gerd Altmann

48

Improvement occurs in performance.

An example of improvement occurring in performance could be a sales team consistently exceeding their monthly targets due to implementing new sales strategies and refining their approach to customer engagement.

49

Correction is achieved in mechanisms.

For instance a manufacturing company identifying and fixing a flaw in their production process, leading to a significant reduction in defects and improved product quality.

Courtesy of Clker Vector

50

Transformation should be disruptive to the structure.

An illustration of this concept could be seen when a traditional brick-and-mortar retailer shifts to an online-only business model, completely restructuring its organization and operations to thrive in the digital marketplace.

Courtesy of Cottonbro studio

51 A paradigm shift leads to a rearrangement of goal prioritization.

An illustration of this could be a company in the automotive industry transitioning its focus from internal combustion engine vehicles to electric vehicles. This paradigm shift would prompt the company to reassess its goals, prioritizing the development of electric vehicle technology and infrastructure while reducing investments in traditional combustion engine technologies.

52

Embracing revolutionary changes can lead to the establishment of new management objectives and values.

It's crucial for management to effectively communicate the rationale behind these shifts, engage employees in the transition process, and provide the necessary support and resources to ensure successful implementation. By embracing change and actively shaping the new direction, management can position the organization for long-term success in a dynamic environment.

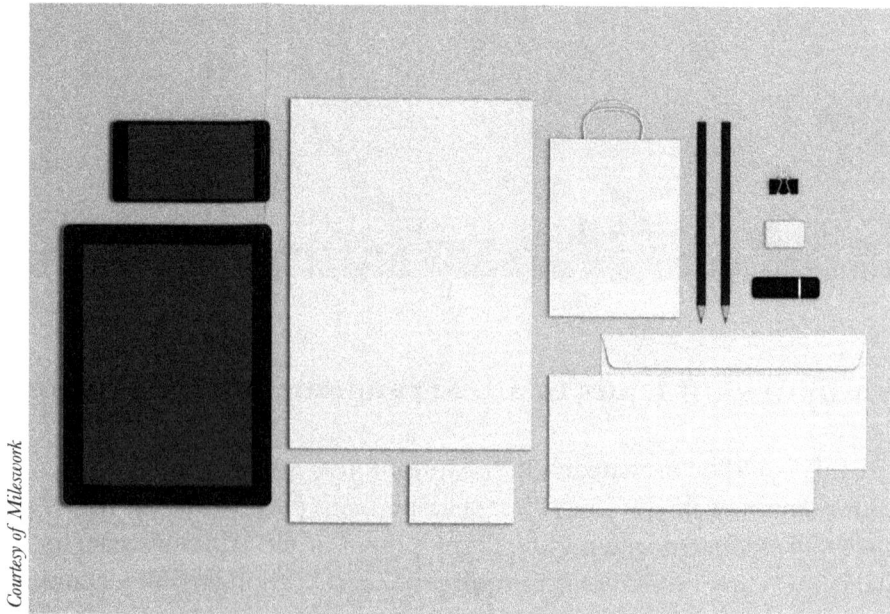

Courtesy of Mileswork

Courtesy of Kindel Media

53

The levels of issues consist of: dilemmas, deadlocks, and crises.

Dilemmas arise when decision-makers confront conflicting choices, requiring careful consideration to navigate effectively. Deadlocks occur when progress halts due to impasses or stalemates, necessitating creative problem-solving techniques or mediation to break through. Crises represent urgent and often unforeseen challenges that demand immediate attention and decisive action to mitigate their impact. Understanding and addressing these various levels of issues are essential for effective management and problem-solving in any context.

54

It's crucial to recognize that genuine insights exist within the minds of individuals, and each component of a structure holds significance independently.

Understanding this principle can guide effective leadership strategies, encouraging managers to value the diverse perspectives and ideas of their team members. By fostering an environment where every element of a project or organization is acknowledged and respected, leaders can harness the full potential of their team, leading to innovative solutions and sustainable growth.

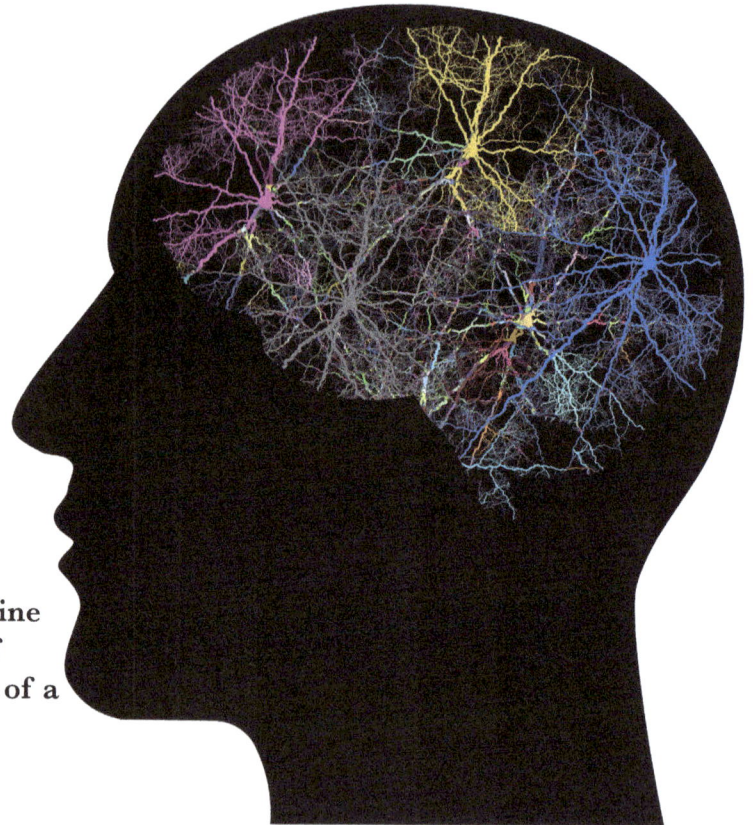

Courtesy of Gordon Johnson

55

Having the courage to gather and disseminate information about ourselves, as shared by customers and competitors, is essential in today's business landscape.

Embracing feedback, whether positive or constructive, enables us to gain valuable insights into our strengths and areas for improvement.

Courtesy of Gerd Altmann

56

Development entails collective learning, which leads to an enhancement of problem-solving capabilities.

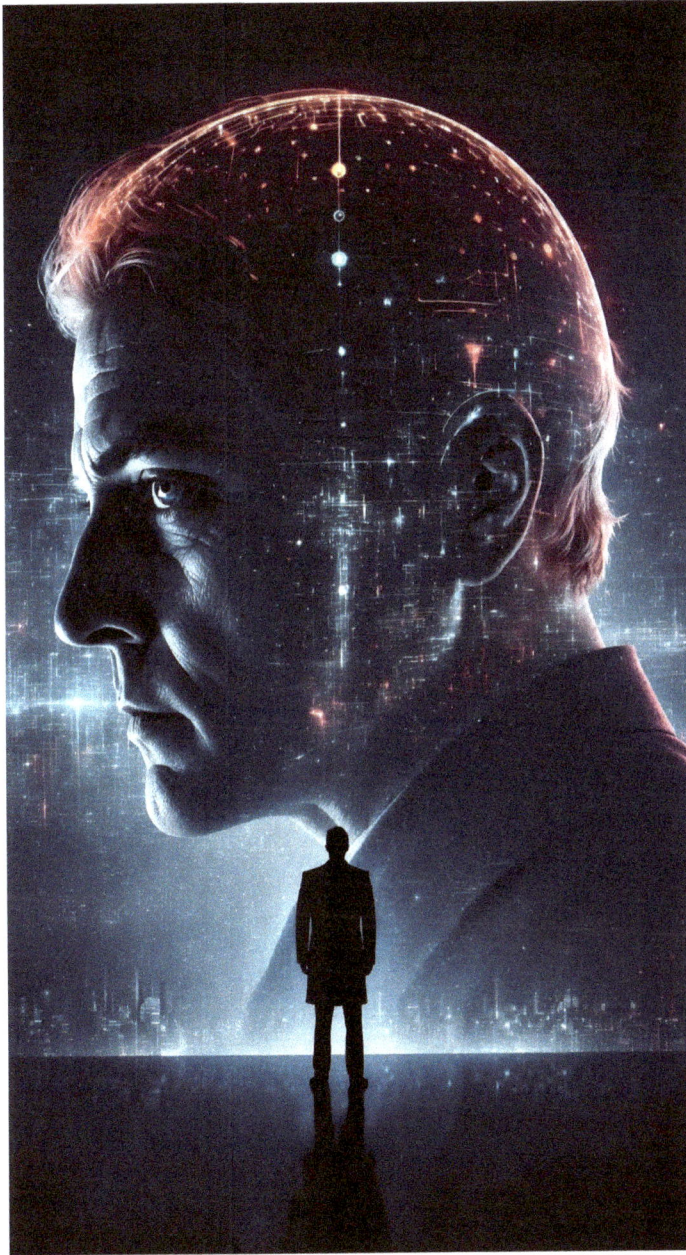

Courtesy of Nicky Pe

57

For individual learning, it's essential for the individual's mental model to align with the beliefs and value system of the organizational framework.

58

The collective mental model within society should translate into societal problem-solving solutions, enabling individual minds to transition from individual intellect to collective wisdom.

Courtesy of Bestpixels

59

Advanced organizations with a high level of maturity place significant value on fostering a culture of open-mindedness and innovation within the workplace.

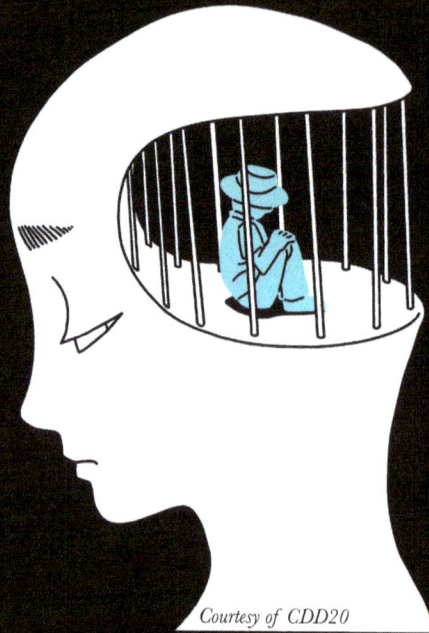

Courtesy of CDD20

60

Development based on temporary and non-sustainable social and economic shocks is transient and unstable.

61

Attention to the limitations of analytical tools and the expertise of specialists is crucial.

Courtesy of Junah Rosales

62

By promoting evidence-based knowledge and combating superstition within the organization, we can prevent the emergence of pseudo-scientific phenomena.

Courtesy of Aleksandar Pasarid

63

Efforts should be directed towards addressing biological needs, as outlined in Maslow's hierarchy of needs, within the organization.

Aligning with Maslow's hierarchy, organizations should prioritize fulfilling employees' biological needs, such as safety, fair compensation, and access to essentials like food and rest. Meeting these basics lays the groundwork for higher-level needs fulfillment, fostering a supportive work environment and boosting morale, engagement, and productivity.

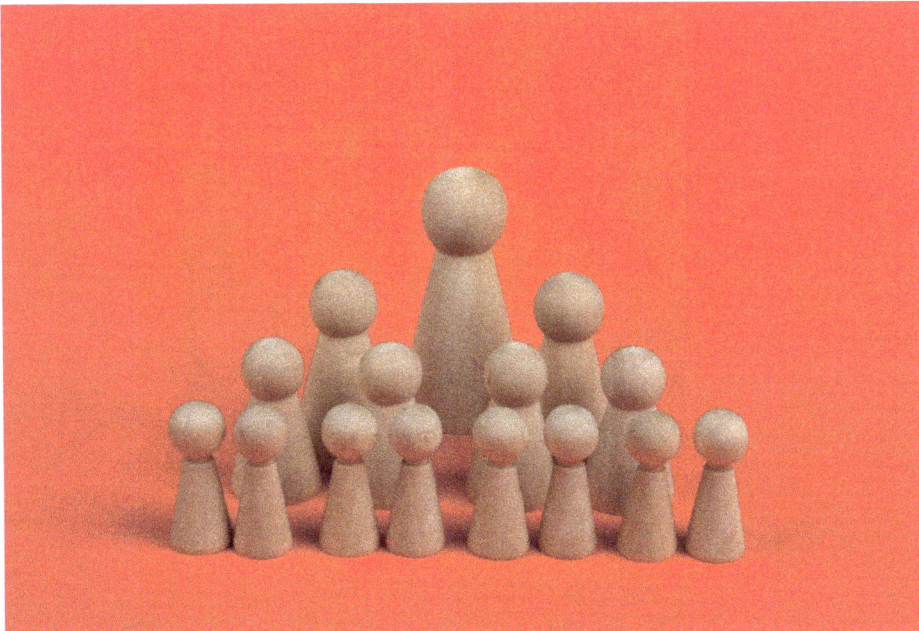

Courtesy of Ann H

64

Facilitate purposeful conversations to nurture the development of experts within the organization.

By implementing structured knowledge-sharing sessions and mentoring programs, we can cultivate an environment where experts within the organization actively engage in purposeful discussions. For instance, hosting regular workshops where experienced professionals share insights and best practices can empower junior staff to learn from their expertise. Additionally, establishing mentorship relationships between seasoned leaders and emerging talent provides a platform for targeted guidance and skill development.

Courtesy of RF._.studio

Courtesy of Fauxels

65

Support reformist groups within the organization that advocate for changes.

they can play a crucial role in driving positive change and innovation. These groups often bring fresh perspectives, identify areas for improvement, and propose solutions to address inefficiencies or outdated practices. By backing these initiatives, organizations demonstrate a commitment to adaptability, responsiveness, and continuous improvement. Additionally, supporting reformist groups can foster a culture of empowerment and engagement among employees, encouraging them to actively contribute to the organization's evolution and success.

Courtesy of Nattanan Kanchanaprat

66

Enhance the organization's capacity by transforming tacit knowledge into explicit knowledge. Ensure that experiences are effectively extracted, documented, and passed on to younger talents within the organization. Don't overlook the valuable insights and contributions of retirees in this process.

67

Enhance organizational sensitivity towards the presence of corruption.

Courtesy of Ekrulila

Courtesy of Anna Nekrashevich

68

The organizational education system requires institutional incentives.

An organizational education system could be the establishment of a performance-based promotion system. Employees who actively engage in training programs, acquire new skills, and contribute to the organization's goals could be rewarded with promotions, salary increases, or other benefits. This incentivizes continuous learning and professional development within the organization.

69

Managers, upon entering a company, prepare employees for accepting a major change by implementing a series of smaller changes.

New managers entering a company may prepare employees for a major change, like transitioning to a new project management system, by first introducing smaller changes. For instance, they might start with new communication tools or minor workflow adjustments. As employees adjust, they gradually introduce larger changes, like training on the new system.

This step-by-step approach helps minimize resistance and ensures successful adoption.

Courtesy of Cottonbro Studio

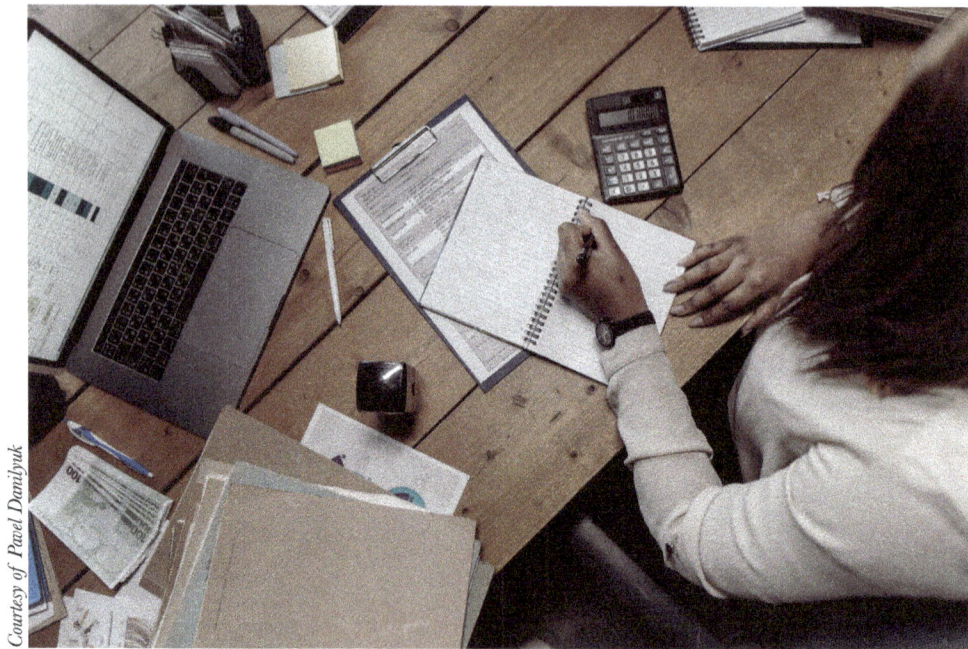

70

Avoid calculator mistakes, or be cautious of calculator errors.

Avoiding calculator mistakes implies taking proactive measures to prevent errors by double-checking calculations, using reliable sources, and verifying results before finalizing them. It emphasizes the importance of accuracy and diligence in mathematical tasks.

On the other hand, being cautious of calculator errors suggests maintaining awareness of the possibility of mistakes and being vigilant in catching and correcting them when they occur. It emphasizes the need for a critical approach to calculations, including verifying inputs and outputs and being attentive to potential sources of error.

71

In various industries, the challenge often resides not in production management but in effective supply chain management.

For instance, in industries like automotive, the main challenge isn't production but ensuring a steady supply of key components, like lithium-ion batteries for electric vehicles.

Courtesy of Pixabay

Courtesy of José Augusto Camargo

72

Let's not diminish values in order to reduce costs.

When managing costs, prioritize retaining value over short-term savings.
Cutting corners can damage reputation and competitiveness in the long
run.

73

You can manage what is measurable, so prioritize the quantifiable aspects of the work.

This approach provides clarity, enables data-driven decision-making, ensures accountability, supports continuous improvement, and optimizes resource allocation.

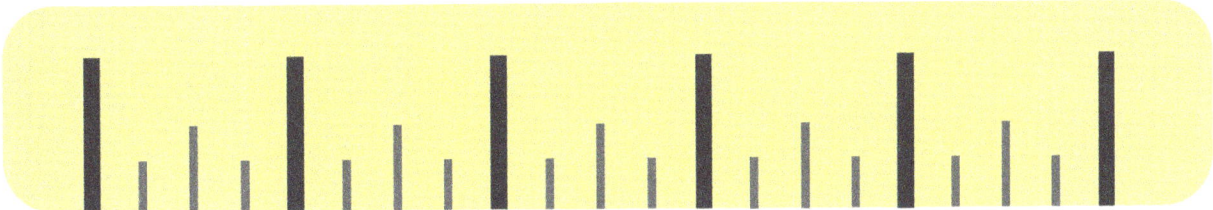

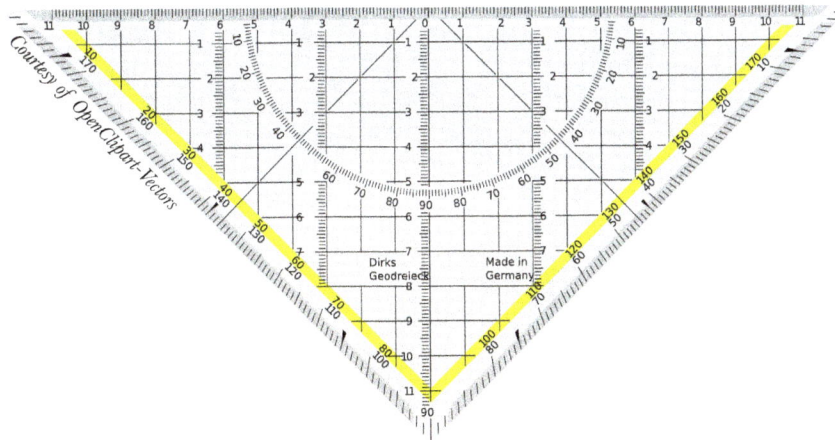

74 **Creating value through preserving value is more important.**

Prioritize preserving existing value while creating new value to ensure sustainability, manage risks, maintain customer satisfaction, build a foundation for growth, and adopt a long-term perspective.

Courtesy of Mohamed Hassan

75 There's a difference between doing good work and doing work well.

Doing good work meets basic requirements, while doing work well exceeds expectations and demonstrates excellence.

QUANTITY

QUALITY

Courtesy of Mohamed Hassan

76 Not adhering to the rules of the game, results in becoming isolated.

If management neglects to follow established rules and ethical standards, it risks legal troubles, reputation damage, employee disengagement, loss of stakeholder trust, and isolation within the industry.

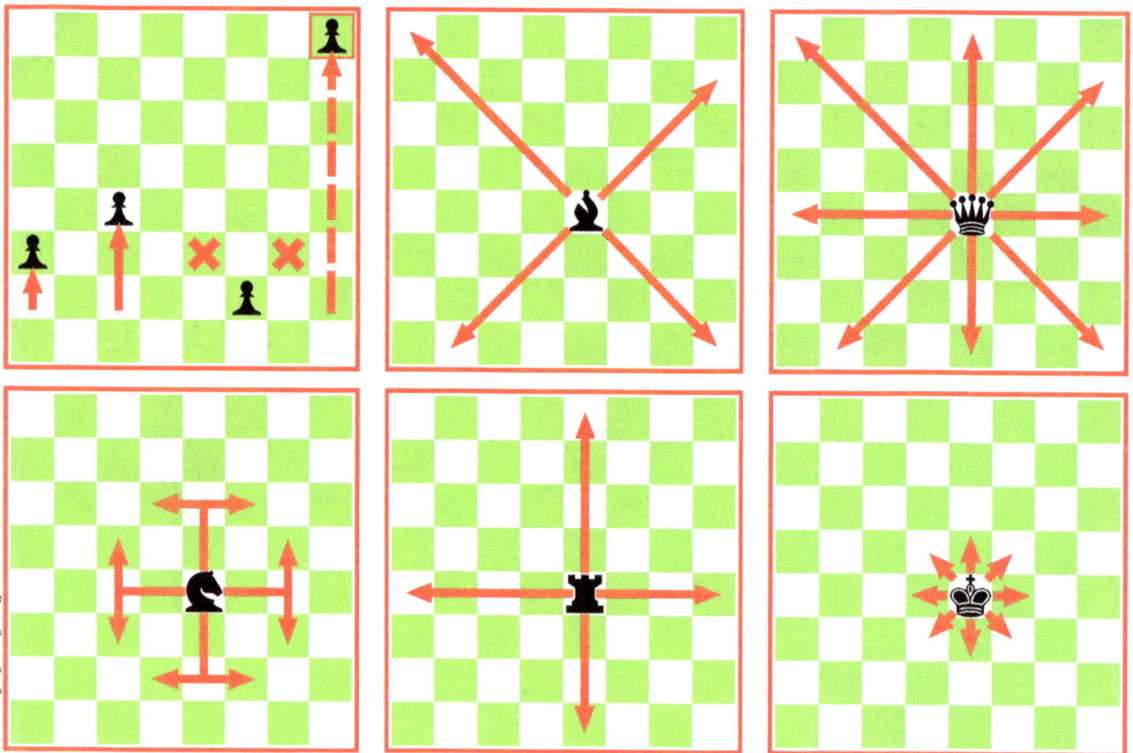

11 Tools alone don't solve the problem.

Consider an example of a project management tool. While such software can help organize tasks, track progress, and facilitate communication, it cannot address underlying issues such as poor planning, ineffective team collaboration, or unclear goals. These issues require human intervention, strategic thinking, and effective leadership to identify and resolve.

Courtesy of Miguel A. Padriñá

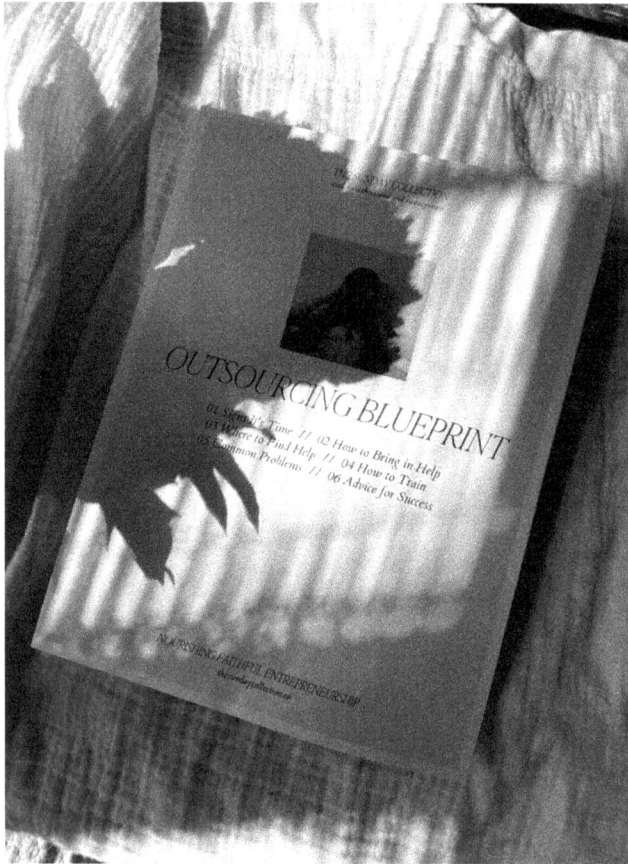
Courtesy of Kiersten Williams

78

You can't outsource your competitive advantage.

Competitive advantages come from unique resources, like technology or talent, integral to a company's identity. While outsourcing can cut costs and boost efficiency, it can't build or maintain these advantages. Over-reliance on outsourcing risks weakening a company's core strengths and control over its business.

79

You can't play every game in every field.

Focus on strategic priorities and specialization to maximize impact. Allocate resources wisely and manage risk effectively. Stay agile and adapt to changes in the business landscape.

Courtesy of Nadim Shaikh

80 Implement ideas based on realities and capabilities.

81 In an organization, fairness should prevail, not equality.

It's crucial to prioritize fairness over strict equality because it acknowledges individual differences and circumstances. While equality aims for uniform treatment, fairness ensures that decisions are just and considerate of all stakeholders, taking into account factors such as merit, need, and contribution.

Created by Midjourney

82 Steer the organization towards embracing both control and flexibility.

Courtesy of Mohamed Hassan

Ensures a balanced approach to operations, allowing for efficiency and adaptability. This approach enables the organization to maintain stability while also being responsive to changes and opportunities in the business environment.

83 Drive the organization towards uniformity so that objectives align. Otherwise, each department sets its own goals, leading to inconsistent systems and wasted energy towards conflicting objectives.

Courtesy of Mohamed Hassan

84 Be mindful of premature aging in the organization. Whether it's due to genetics or poor nutrition.

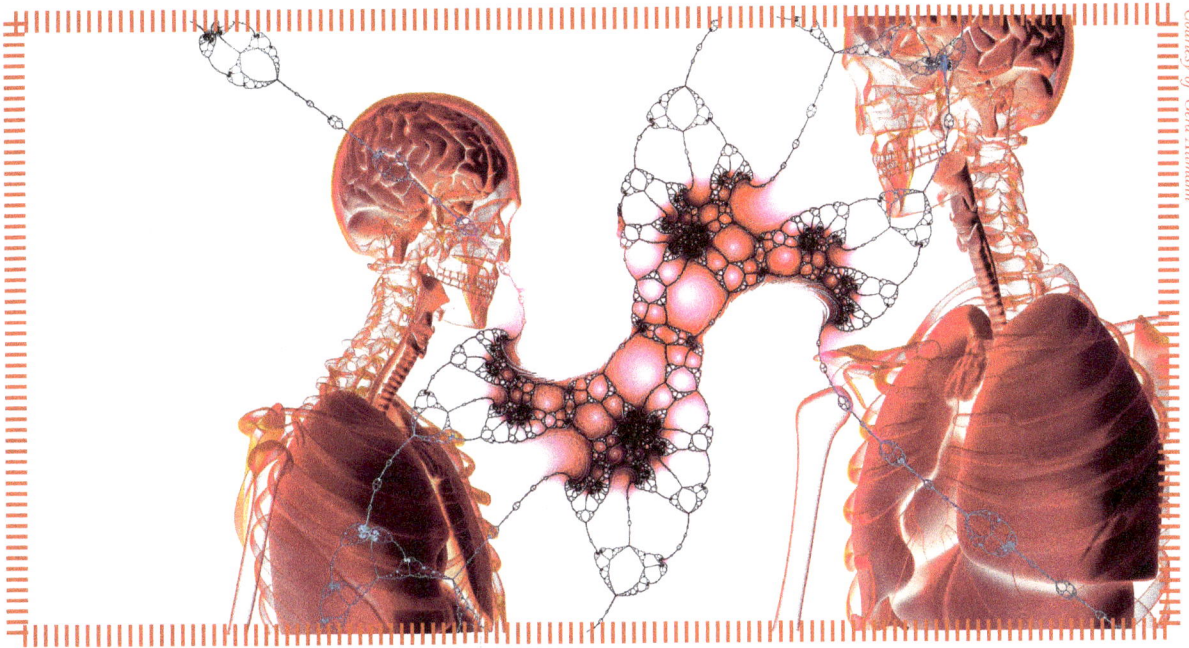

Courtesy of Gerd Altmann

85 The laws governing the cell override its structure.

In management, regulatory compliance takes precedence over organizational structure.

86

If society's cells exhibit cohesive behavior in the face of shocks, they demonstrate unity and a shared purpose.

When cells in a society demonstrate cohesive behavior during challenges, it indicates a sense of unity and shared goals among its members. This cohesion can foster resilience, collaboration, and collective action, enabling the society to navigate challenges more effectively and achieve common objectives.

Courtesy of Collective Studio

87

During periods of rapid growth and maturity, be mindful of the 'valley of death' stages in startup development. Recognize the risks associated with founders' dominance, leadership transitions, prolonged tensions, and unexpected events. Proactively address challenges to ensure the long-term sustainability and success of the organization.

Courtesy of Ruslan Bahiba

Several stages occur after rapid growth:

- **Founders' Dominance and Ejection of Transformational Managers:** Founders often assert dominance, leading to the expulsion of managers advocating for significant changes.
- **The Dominance of Young Managers and Founders' Retreat:** Young managers take control as founders step back or become less involved in day-to-day operations.
- **Prolonged Tension Leading to Bankruptcy:** Tensions may escalate and persist, ultimately leading to bankruptcy due to unresolved conflicts or mismanagement
- **Accidental Death of Founders:** In some cases, the accidental death of founders may occur, further complicating the startup's trajectory and future.

Courtesy of Andrea Piacquadio

88

Pursue a system for attracting top talent to accelerate growth and evolution.

89 Micro-level competition hampers progress, promoting cutthroat behavior. Collaborative competition fosters excellence through teamwork and shared goals.

90

A productive society possesses four key traits:

- Patience for collaboration
- Happiness
- High social capital
- Self-confidence

Courtesy of Dương Nhân

91

Transparency is the first pillar. It means being clear and honest about what's going on.

92

An increase in energy consumption intensity within an organization indicates structural waste.

Courtesy of Hasan Albari

93

The difference in each organization lies in its objectives

94 A non-rentier system aligns with capability.

Courtesy of mykhailo_kolisnyk

95 Sanctions act as a catalyst for crisis.
There's a crisis reserve waiting to explode.

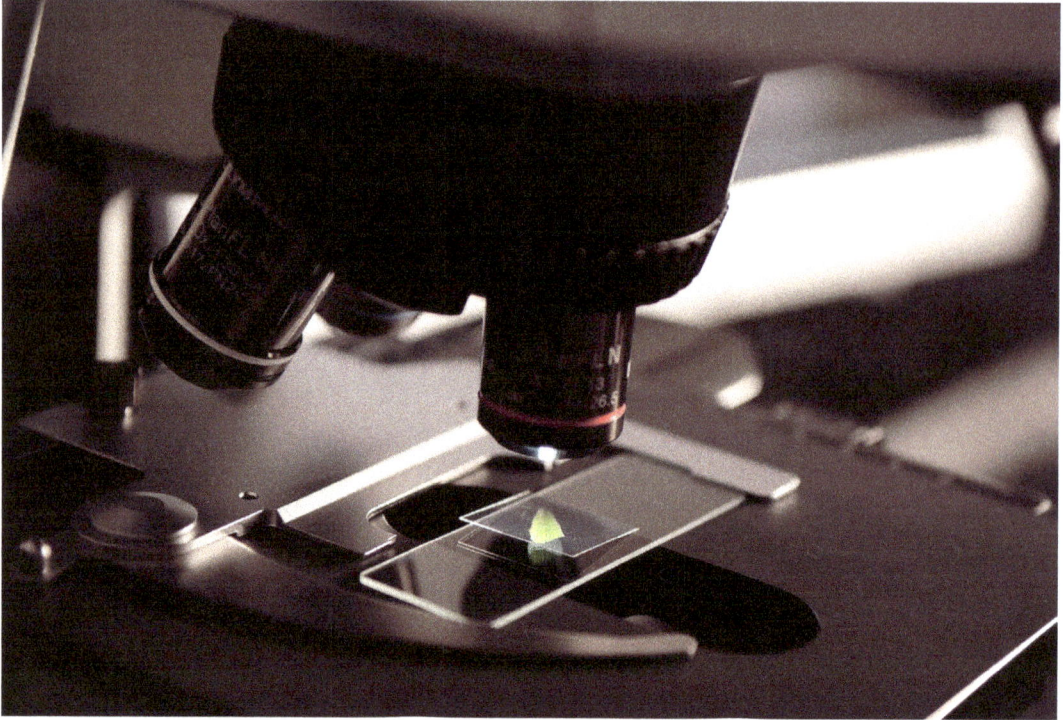

Courtesy of Pixabay

96 **Analyze information within its relevant context for more accurate insights.**

97 Ensure accurate analysis by avoiding broad generalizations. Utilize globally recognized indices, such as the Big Mac Index or the McDonald's Index, for effective measurement and analysis.

Courtesy of Olavi Anttila

98

To truly understand a culture, one must immerse oneself in its environment. Managers need to familiarize themselves with the native culture of their employees to gain a multifaceted perspective on the cultural environment.

Courtesy of Los Muertos Crew

Revenue

Courtesy of aroblesgalit

99

Watch out for the fallacy of linear extrapolation. Not every graph necessarily indicates slow growth, even if it previously followed a growth trajectory, like a child growth chart.

"Be cautious of assuming linear growth trends; not all graphs follow a steady path, similar to child growth charts which indicate growth spurts and plateaus."
The significance of child growth charts lies in their ability to track a child's physical development over time, helping identify potential health concerns or abnormalities.

100

Mastering 99% of the various aspects of a problem is the essence of problem-solving intelligence.

By thoroughly exploring different dimensions of the problem, individuals can identify key challenges, anticipate potential obstacles, and devise more informed and strategic solutions. Problem-solving intelligence encompasses the ability to navigate complex problems by considering various factors, perspectives, and potential outcomes.

Courtesy of Hanne Hasu

CHANGE NOW 99%

Courtesy of Sumanley xulx

101

The simplest approach may not always be the most accurate.

Complex problems often require thorough analysis and consideration of multiple factors. While a simple solution may seem appealing, it may overlook important nuances or intricacies that could affect the outcome.

$$\frac{F}{M}$$

www.ingramcontent.com/pod-product-compliance
Lightning Source LLC
Chambersburg PA
CBHW051759200326

41597CB00025B/4611